W9-AUJ-234

AMERICAN CARS
THROUGH THE DECADES

American Cars
of the 1990s and Today

Craig Cheetham

McLean County Unit #5
112-Sugar Creek

GARETH**STEVENS**
GS
PUBLISHING
A Member of the WRC Media Family of Companies

Please visit our web site at: www.garethstevens.com
For a free color catalog describing Gareth Stevens Publishing's
list of high-quality books and multimedia programs,
call 1-800-542-2595 (USA) or 1-800-387-3178 (Canada).
Gareth Stevens Publishing's fax: (414) 332-3567.

Library of Congress Cataloging-in-Publication Data

Cheetham, Craig.
    American cars of the 1990s and today / Craig Cheetham.
       p. cm. — (American cars through the decades)
    Includes bibliographical references and index.
    ISBN-13: 978-0-8368-7728-1 (lib. bdg.)
    1. Automobiles—United States—History. I. Title.
TL23.C444   2007
629.2220973—dc22   2006051087

This North American edition first published in 2007 by
Gareth Stevens Publishing
A Member of the WRC Media Family of Companies
330 West Olive Street, Suite 100
Milwaukee, WI 53212 USA

Produced by Amber Books Ltd., Bradley's Close,
74–77 White Lion Street, London N1 9PF, U.K.

Project Editor: Michael Spilling
Design: Joe Conneally

Gareth Stevens managing editor: Valerie J. Weber
Gareth Stevens editor: Alan Wachtel
Gareth Stevens art direction: Tammy West
Gareth Stevens cover design: Dave Kowalski
Gareth Stevens production: Jessica Yanke and Robert Kraus

Illustrations and photographs copyright International Masters
Publishers AB/Aerospace–Art-Tech

Printed in the United States of America

1 2 3 4 5 6 7 8 9 10 10 09 08 07 06

Table of Contents

AM General Hummer

The Hummer was first built for the U.S. military. It is is now a popular car among wealthy drivers.

The Hummer comes with either a gasoline engine or a diesel engine. The U.S. Army uses Hummers with diesel **V-8** engines.

Hummers are very wide. This helps them remain stable as they turn, especially on rough roads.

No parts of the vehicle stick out at the front or rear, which helps the Hummer get over obstacles.

The car is built on a separate steel **chassis** that is not welded into the structure of the body.

This Hummmer is taking part in a cross-country race through the Nevada Desert.

1983

The U.S. Army begins using Hummers.

1992

Hummer becomes part of General Motors, and the cars go on sale to the public.

Hummers are all-purpose vehicles that can go almost anywhere. They first appeared in the early 1980s. At that time, only the U.S. military used them.

High Rider

The body of the Hummer sits more than 16 inches (40.6 centimeters) above the ground. Its **suspension** gives it 9 inches (22.8 cm) of ground clearance. This means the Hummer can easily travel over broken roads and rough country without its body hitting obstacles.

Hummers went on sale to the public in 1992 after appearing regularly on television during the Gulf War. They are known in the military as "Humvees," from the initials HMMWV spoken very fast. The initials stand for "High Mobility Multi-purpose Wheeled Vehicle."

UNDER THE SKIN

The Hummer was built to be tough. Its strong chassis is almost unbreakable.

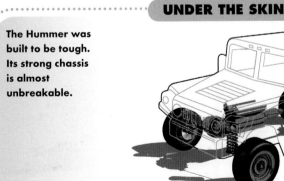

Cadillac Catera

The Catera was Cadillac's answer to European luxury cars on sale in the U.S. It was, in fact, based on a European design called the Opel.

The Catera's lights went all the way across the trunk lid. This style was very different than the Opel's.

The Catera was a small car, but its Cadillac **grille** showed that it was made by the company known for large, fancy cars.

The car's cabin included high-quality leather seats.

Under the hood, the Catera had a 3.0-liter (184-cubic-inch) **V-6** engine that was designed in Germany.

The Catera could **accelerate** from 0 to 60 miles (96 km) per hour in 8.5 seconds.

1994

General Motors launches the Opel and the Vauxhall Omega (pictured below) in Europe.

1996

The Catera makes its debut in the United States.

In the mid 1990s, many people stopped buying Cadillacs and started buying smaller European models instead.

To win them back, Cadillac turned to its parent company, General Motors, for help. GM sold a model of car in Europe called the Opel and the Vauxhall Omega. The Cadillac now began offering a car like these models in the United States as the Cadillac Catera.

Luxury Ride

Its **luxury** ride, good build, and lively performance were exactly what Cadillac buyers wanted, so it sold well.

The Catera was smaller than most Cadillac cars, but American buyers liked it all the same.

UNDER THE SKIN

The Cadillac Catera has a special rear supension to deal with heavy loads.

7

Cadillac STS Seville

The Seville was Cadillac's top model, and it sold all over the world.

The interior of the Seville featured a **navigation system**, a CD player, and power seats.

The Seville's square shape went well with Cadillac's distinctive grille.

The car's big headlights were typical of Cadillac style.

The car's trunk and hood were about the same size.

The car came with **alloy** wheels in a chrome or satin finish.

Many people thought the Seville was an attractive car.

1997

Cadillac announces its new Seville.

1998

The company sells the Seville throughout Europe, including a **right-hand drive** model in Great Britain.

In the 1990s, many buyers began to prefer smaller cars. There was, however, still a demand for the large, luxury models that were the most important part of Cadillac's business.

Luxury Model

The Seville was a luxury Cadillac. The inside was big and comfortable. It also had many electronic gadgets — including climate control and a good music system — and leather seats. The Seville was considered a good value because it was cheaper than similar cars from Jaguar, BMW, and Mercedes-Benz. It also sold well in Europe, making it Cadillac's first successful model outside the United States.

UNDER THE SKIN

The Seville's sophisticated suspension offers great comfort. It also handles well on the road.

Chevrolet Camaro SS

The Camaro was already a great car, but the SS version was the best of all the Camaro models.

The Camaro SS's **exhaust pipe** was sports tuned, so it gave out a throaty roar.

The Camaro SS was heavier at the front than the back, making it slide easily in wet weather.

It was easy to tell a Camaro SS from another Camaro model by its black roof.

Inside, the Camaro SS was a perfect blend of **sports car** and luxury car.

The car's special five-spoke alloy wheels had a red Chevrolet logo in the center.

Fast but also safe, the Camaro SS had powerful brakes that could bring it to a stop in a short distance.

MILESTONES

1996

A tuning company called Street Legal Performance offers SS packages on Camaro Z28s.

1998

Chevrolet makes the SS a standard production model in its Camaro line.

The Chevrolet Camaro Z28 was popular among car fans. It was cheap and very, very fast. Some buyers, however, wanted an even faster Camaro. Chevrolet's response to them was the Camaro SS.

Superfast

The Camaro SS had different front-end styling than the Z28 and a black top to make it stand out. The car's V-8 engine put out 320 horsepower. It accelerated from 0 to 60 miles (96 km) per hour in 5.2 seconds and reached a top speed of 160 miles (257 km) per hour. Chevrolet built fewer than 8,000 Camaro SS models in 1998.

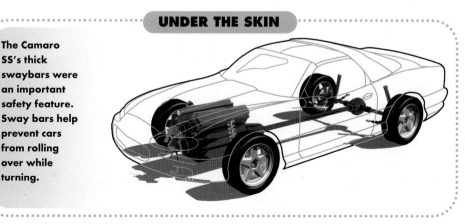

UNDER THE SKIN

The Camaro SS's thick swaybars were an important safety feature. Sway bars help prevent cars from rolling over while turning.

Chevrolet Corvette GS

The Corvette Grand Sport (GS) was the last Corvette model made before the line was completely redesigned, and it had a unique look.

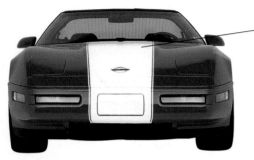

The Grand Sport was available in only one color — metallic admiral blue — and it had a white stripe over the front and back.

The hood opens forward, giving good access to the engine bay.

The car's roof panel could be taken off, so the Grand Sport was both a **coupe** and a **convertible**.

All Grand Sports had a six-speed **stick-shift transmission**.

The Grand Sport's black wheels gave it a mean look.

The Grand Sport's bright blue and white paint job gives it the look of a racer.

1990

People get their first chance to see the Corvette ZR-1.

1996

Chevrolet launches the Grand Sport to mark the end of the fourth-generation Corvette.

In 1996, Chevrolet was about to redesign the Corvette. Before doing so, to celebrate the earlier Corvettes, the company offered a limited edition — the Grand Sport. The Grand Sport was based on the top-of-the-line Corvette ZR-1.

One Color

It came only in admiral blue, the same color as Chevrolet's famous 1960s Sting Ray racers. Power came from a 350-cubic-inch (5,735-cubic-centimeter) V-8 engine, which put out 330 **horsepower**. The Grand Sport could accelerate from 0 to 60 miles (96 km) per hour in 4.7 seconds, and then on to a top speed of almost 170 miles (273.5 km) per hour. Chevrolet built only 1,000 Grand Sports, making it a very popular model among Corvette collectors today.

UNDER THE SKIN

Like all Corvettes before it, the Grand Sport was made out of fiberglass. This made the car light and helped it go faster.

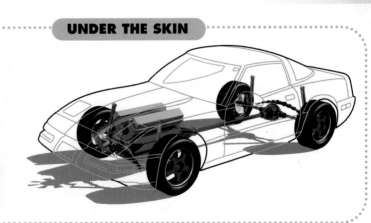

13

Chrysler Sebring

The Sebring was a luxury sports car that quickly became popular.

The Sebring was available in both hardtop and convertible versions.

On Sebring convertible models, the seat-belt reels were attached to the car's seats.

Top-of-the-line "Limited" Sebring models had leather-trimmed interiors and chrome-alloy wheels.

The Sebring had a fuel-saving gasoline engine. The Japanese car company Mitsubishi helped to develop it.

The top of the Sebring convertible could be lowered in just ten seconds.

1995

Chrysler introduced new **sedans**, including the Cirrus and Stratus. The Sebring (below) was based on those models.

1996

The Sebring convertible makes its debut.

In the 1990s, Chrysler was facing strong competition from European car companies. Chrysler knew it had to make its 1990s sports-car models **fuel-efficient** and affordable, as well as fast and attractive.

High Praise

When Chrysler launched the Sebring in 1995, many people praised it for being one of the best-looking cars in its class. Inside, the car had a smooth, curvy dashboard, leather seats, and lots of space for passengers.

The Sebring was a huge success for Chrysler. Its fresh look helped it stay in production, with very few changes, until 2003.

UNDER THE SKIN

The Sebring's V6 engine was mounted near the center of the car to prevent the car from being too heavy at its front.

Dodge Ram V-10

*Pickup trucks are popular in the United States today —
and the RAM V-10 is the mightiest of them all.*

The Ram's big grille gives
it the appearance of a
scaled-down big truck.

The Ram's **V-10** engine is based
on the Dodge Viper's engine and
produces 300 horsepower.

The Ram's **rollbar** makes the truck
safer, and it is also a good place
to attach extra lights.

The Ram's cabin is as
luxurious as a car's,
with comfortable seats,
air-conditioning, and a
CD player.

Pictures cannot show just how large the Ram is. At 6 feet, 5 inches (1.96 meters), it is one-and-one-half times as tall as a normal sedan car.

MILESTONES

1994
Dodge launches the bold-looking Ram, which has the most luxurious interior of any pickup truck.

2004
The company introduces the more powerful, restyled Ram V-10.

The Dodge Ram V-10 is not for the quiet or the shy. It is Dodge's top-of-the-line pickup truck, and it is a huge and bold-looking truck. It drives like a car, however, and Dodge also makes a **double-cab** version that has the same amount of space inside as a sedan.

Big Engine, Big Noise
The Ram is the first American pickup truck to use a V-10 engine. It is noisy, but some people like its powerful sound.

The Ram is popular in the United States — 12 percent of full-size trucks sold in the country are Dodge Ram V-10s. The big disadvantage of owning a Ram V-10, however, is that it uses a lot of gas. The Ram V-10 is not cheap to run.

UNDER THE SKIN

When it came on the market, the Ram was the only American pickup truck that had a V-10 engine.

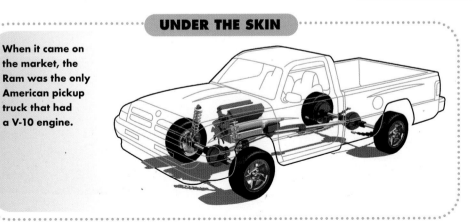

Dodge Viper 1992

The Viper is the most famous American supercar of recent years.

The Viper's body panels were made out of fiberglass to keep the car as light as possible.

The rollbar was built into the Viper's body to blend in with the car's smooth styling.

The Viper had cutaway sections in front of its doors to let heat escape from the engine.

Under the hood, the Viper had a V-10 engine. It was the only production car of its time to have such a huge engine.

The Viper had three-spoke alloy wheels.

The Viper can accelerate from 0 to 60 miles (96 km) per hour in just 4.2 seconds.

MILESTONES

1992

Dodge delivers the first Vipers to customers three years after the company first showed the design at the Detroit Auto Show.

1996

Dodge launches a hardtop version of the Viper — the GTS-R — that performed even better than the original.

Dodge did not know whether to build the Viper or not, so the company showed a drawing of it at the Detroit Auto Show in 1989. Car buyers loved the design, so Dodge went ahead and built it. The result was one of the most legendary cars of the 1990s.

Power Car

The Viper looked and sounded amazing. The car got its power from a 400-horsepower V-10 engine, and it had a top speed of 160 miles (257 km) per hour. It also handled well. For many supercar fans, the Viper was the equal of the best models made by Ferrari and Porsche.

UNDER THE SKIN

The Viper's tubular steel frame was very strong, keeping the car steady at high speeds.

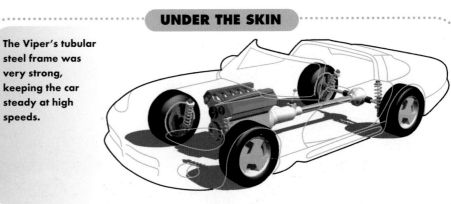

Ford F-150

The best-selling vehicle in the United States today is not a car. It is the Ford F-150 — a pickup truck.

F-150 buyers have a choice of a V-6 or a V-8 engine.

The F-150's heavy-duty chassis makes the truck tough and safe.

The F-150 is available with either a **single-cab** (shown here) or a double-cab. The double-cab version can seat six people.

The F-150's grille is similar to the one on Ford's LTD Sedan.

The F-150 Lightning is the fastest, most luxurious version of Ford's bestselling pickup truck.

1995

Ford launches the current generation F-150.

2002

The F-150 gets a major restyling for the twenty-first century.

The Ford F-150 is the best-selling vehicle in the United States, proving that many Americans love pickup trucks. Ford sells more than one million F-150s each year.

Dual Purpose

The F-150 is a dual-purpose vehicle. It has the cargo space of a truck's bed combined with the comfort of a car. Even the F-150s that can seat six people have huge cargo areas. Some F-150 owners use the truck like a family car. But it can still be put to work by those who need a truck for carrying heavy loads. One of the main reasons the F-150 is so popular is that it is a good value for the money. It costs only a little more than a Ford Focus, a popular budget sedan.

UNDER THE SKIN

The F-150 has a simple chassis. Buyers can choose between two or four-wheel-drive models.

Ford Mustang Cobra R

With the Cobra R, Ford took the Mustang to new heights in the 1990s.

The hood was made out of lightweight fiberglass to keep the car's weight down.

The Cobra R's styling included a big bulge on the hood and a sporty rear **spoiler**.

Cobra Rs had low-profile tires to keep the car as close to the road as possible.

Inside, the Cobra R had luxury features such as a CD player and leather seats.

The two holes in the car's front spoiler let air flow to the brakes to keep them cool.

This is the coupe version of the Cobra R.

1993
Ford builds the first Mustang Cobra R, based on the old Mustang 5.0L.

1998
The latest, fastest Mustang Cobra R makes its debut.

Ford was allowed to use the Cobra name because the legendary tuner Carroll Shelby, who created the first Shelby Cobra car, also helped to develop the Mustang Cobra R.

With the Mustang Cobra R, Ford's Special Vehicle Team (SVT) built a racing car for the road. The Cobra R's sporty body shape and alloy wheels made it clear that the car was built for speed.

V-8 Shelby Engine
With a 300-horsepower, 351-cubic-inch (5752-cc) V-8 engine under the hood, the Cobra R was fast. It had a top speed of 150 miles (241 km) per hour, and it could accelerate from 0 to 60 miles (96 km) in 5.5 seconds.

UNDER THE SKIN

The V-8 engine was powerful, but it was also an old-fashioned design.

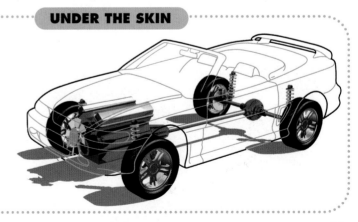

Lincoln Navigator

*As one of the most luxurious **SUVs** on the market, the Navigator is at home in the city as much as it is in the country.*

The Navigator comes with a four-speed automatic transmission.

The rear **tailgate** opens in two sections.

The Navigator has a special grille that looks like a waterfall.

All Navigators were built with safety in mind. The driver and the front seat passenger each have their own airbag.

All Navigators have air springs that the driver can use to adjust the ride height of the car for driving on rough roads.

When driving off road, the Navigator body can be raised by 1 inch (2.5 centimeters) to help it clear rough ground.

MILESTONES

1994

Ford releases the Bronco, which was based on the F-150's chassis.

1998

Lincoln uses the Bronco as the basis for its luxury SUV, the Navigator (pictured below).

leather and wood trim, plus climate control and a stereo system. The Navigator also has an extra seat in the cargo area that enables it to seat seven people.

Lincoln had a long history of building luxury sedans, so many people were surprised when it launched the Navigator, a big SUV. Many American car buyers, however, love four-wheel drive vehicles, and the luxury car maker did not want to miss out on sales. Lincoln's decision was a good one, because the Navigator is now one of the most popular SUVs in the United States.

From the outside, the Navigator looks impressive. Its high nose and chunky tires make it look like it can handle rough roads. Inside, the luxurious cabin has

UNDER THE SKIN

All Navigators have an advanced air suspension.

25

Lincoln Town Car

*With its smooth looks, the Lincoln Town Car
is one of the last luxury sedans.*

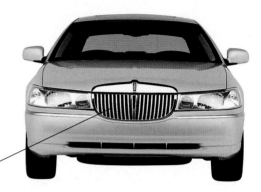

The Town Car's four-door body has
a flat roof that makes the car ideal
for converting into a stretch limo.

All Town Cars have a
4.6-liter (281-cubic-inch)
V-8 engine and an
automatic transmission.

The Town Car has a lot of room
inside. Back seat passengers
have more than 40 inches
(102 cm) of leg space.

As a safety feature, the
Town Car has airbags
at the front and sides
of the front seats.

The Town Car's excellent suspension means passengers and drivers always have a smooth ride.

1998

The all-new Town Car debuts, replacing the square and boxy 1990 model (below).

1999

A special Cartier edition that features many luxury options is launched.

There was a time when full-size cars such as the Lincoln Town Car were common, but changes in driving habits have made many people want either small, sporty models or SUVs. Today, it is unusual to see full-size sedans like the Lincoln Town Car.

Luxury Sedan

Smoothly styled and very comfortable, the Town Car is a luxury car. The dashboard is trimmed with wood, and the leather seats are large. There is lots of leg room for passengers in the back seats, making the Town Car one of the most spacious cars around. Although the car market has changed, the Town Car is popular with many senior citizens and people who prefer a full-size sedan.

UNDER THE SKIN

The Town Car uses the same engine as the Ford Mustang — the V-8.

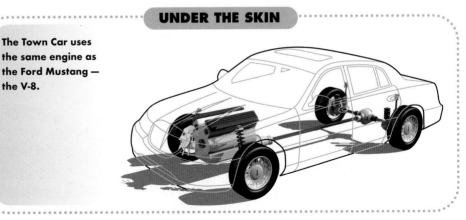

Plymouth Prowler

Plymouth did not plan to produce the Prowler — until it received 100,000 orders.

All of the Prowler's panels, as well as its seat frames and suspension, are made of lightweight aluminum.

The big front bumpers did not fit well with the car's hot-rod styling, but U.S. safety laws required them.

The car's tires were designed so that they could be driven on even if they were flat.

The Prowlers separate mudguards gave it the look of a 1930s custom **hot rod.**

The Prowler's twin tail pipes suggested that it had a huge V-8 engine under its hood, but it had only a smaller V-6.

The Prowler was built out of aluminum to make it as light as possible. Because of its light body, the Prowler was able to go 118 miles (190 km) per hour even though it had a small V-6 engine.

1993
Plymouth shows a Prowler model (below) at the Detroit Auto Show in January.

1997
The Prowler goes on sale. By the time of its launch, it has already sold out.

In the 1990s, few car makers were as popular as Chrysler, which owns both Dodge and Plymouth. Car buyers already thought the 1992 Dodge Viper was amazing. Then, in 1993, the company showed the Plymouth Prowler at the Detroit Auto Show.

By Popular Demand
Chrysler never meant to build the Prowler, but, by the end of the show, it had received orders from more than 100,000 customers who wanted one. The company quickly put the car into production. By law, Chrysler had to add two front bumpers that were not part of the original design to the car. The Prowler came in only one color — metallic purple.

UNDER THE SKIN

The Prowler's alloy panels hid a tube chassis similar to the chassis of a racing car.

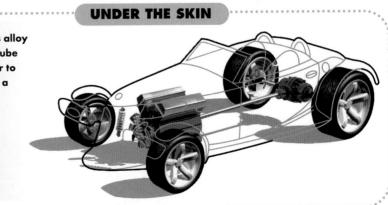

Glossary

accelerate to increase speed

alloy made of two or more metals mixed together

chassis the part of a car body to which the engine, transmission, and suspension are attached

convertible a car with a roof that can be lowered

coupe a two-door car, usually seating only two people

double cab a truck cab featuring two rows of seats

exhaust pipe a metal tube that takes the burned gasses away from an engine and makes it quieter

fiberglass a lightweight material made from glass strands and plastic

four-wheel drive a drive system in a vehicle that sends power to all four of the vehicle's wheels

fuel-efficient able to use a small amount of fuel to produce a relatively large amount of power

grille a guard at the front end of a vehicle that lets in air to cool the engine

horsepower a unit of measure of the power of an engine

hot rod a car that has been modified for extra speed and, often, a sleeker look

luxury special and expensive

navigation system an electronic device that gives a car's location and directions for getting from one place to another

right-hand drive having a steering wheel on the front, right-hand side

rollbars tubes that strengthen the frame of a car, protecting the driver if the car rolls over

sedans closed automobiles with two or four doors and front and rear seats

single cab a vehicle that has only one row of seats

spoiler a device on the front or rear of a vehicle that changes the direction of the flow of air to stop the vehicle from lifting off the road at high speeds

sports car a car with fast performance and stylish looks

stick-shift having a lever that a driver uses a vehicle's transmission

SUVs sport-utility vehicles; large, powerful vehicles that have the space of a small truck and the performance of a good sedan

supercar a fast, luxurious high-performance car

suspension a system of springs at the base of a car's body that keeps a vehicle even on bumpy surfaces

tailgate a board at the rear of a vehicle that can be let down on a hinge or removed

transmission a system in a vehicle that controls the gears, sending power from the engine to the wheels to make them move

tuner a person who adjusts cars to drive faster and steer and stop better

V-6, V-8, V-10 engines that have a number of cylinders arranged opposite each other in a V-shape

For More Information

Books

Big Book of Cars. (DK Publishing)

Car. DK Eyewitness (series). Richard Sutton
   and Elizabeth Baquedano (DK Children)

Cars. All About (series). Peter Harrison (Southwater)

Mega Book of Cars. Mega Books (series).
   (Chrysalis Books)

Racing Cars. Cool Wheels (series). Richard Gunn
   (Gareth Stevens Publishing)

Speed! — Cars. Speed! (series). Jenifer Corr Morse
   (Blackbirch Press)

Sweet Rides. Automania! (series). Katherine Bailey
   (Crabtree Publishing Company)

Web Sites

All Muscle Cars
www.allmusclecars.com

Greatest Engineering Achievements of the 20th Century
   — Automobile
www.greatachievements.org

Museum of Automobile History
www.themuseumofautomobilehistory.com

Dodge Viper Central
www.vipercentral.com/pics/pics.htm

Publishers note to educators and parents:
Our editors have carefully reviewed these Web sites to
ensure that they are suitable for children. Many Web
sites change frequently, however, and we cannot guarantee
that a site's future contents will continue to meet our high
standards of quality and educational value. Be advised
that children should be closely supervised whenever they
access the Internet.

Index